S0-BZK-578

life

with Vimrod

life

life is terribly **long** isn't it?

shall we rest?

Vimrod by Lisa Swerling and Ralph Lazar

**Andrews McMeel
Publishing, LLC**

Kansas City

i find life disconcerting.

may i please have some chocolate
to stabilize myself?

life
starts
messy and
ends
messy.

so how come
we have to
tidy our
bedrooms?

try,
try,
try again.

if still you
don't succeed,
pay for
someone
else to do it.

the only way
to live life is
by breathing
continuously

if life is short
and life's a beach,
how come there are
long beaches?
beach

stream of consciousness is... ...um...
...uh... ...dunno.

is there

any cure for the human condition?

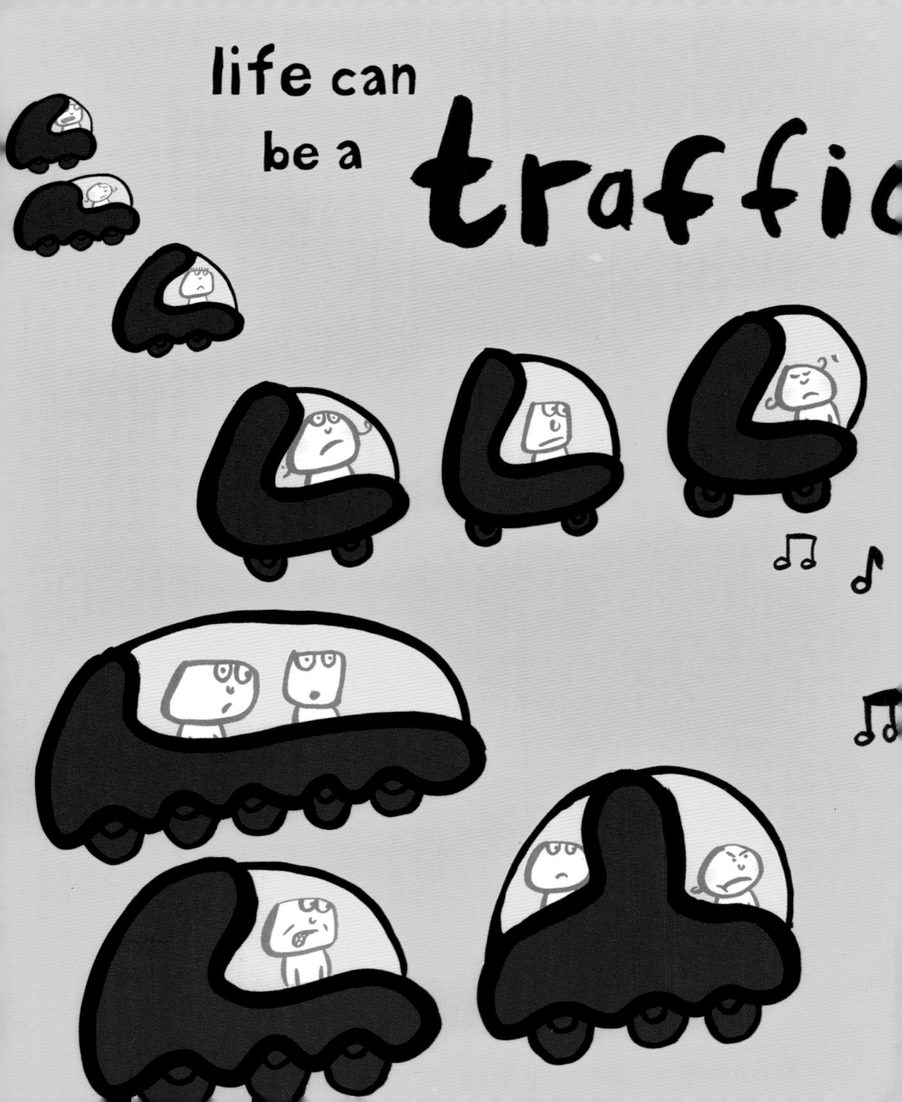
life can
be a traffic

your lack of depression is
making me nervous.

are you ok?

hello,
this is the sky
sky
speaking

yes, the sky.

you are a small speck
on a **huge** planet,
so **stop** taking yourself
so seriously.

life is

just a journey

offices,

isn't it?

really between

office C

office E

office F

office I

there are times in your life when you have money,

and there are times when you don't have money.

then there are times when you don't have money,

and then times when you still don't have money.

lisa swerling + ralph lazar

are two of the UK's most popular graphic artists. Through their company Last Lemon they have brought to life a range of inspired cartoon characters, including Harold's Planet, The Brainwaves, Blessthischick and, of course, Vimrod.

Writers, artists, and designers, they are married with two children, and spend their time between London and various beaches around the world.

ISBN-13: 978-0-7407-7809-4

ISBN-10: 0-7407-7809-9

09 10 11 12 13 SDB 10 9 8 7 6 5 4 3 2 1

The authors assert the moral right to be identified as the authors of this work.

www.vimrod.com

www.andrewsmcmeel.com

ATTENTION: SCHOOLS AND BUSINESSES

Andrews McMeel books are available at quantity discounts with bulk purchase for educational, business, or sales promotional use. For information, please write to: Special Sales Department, Andrews McMeel Publishing, LLC, 1130 Walnut Street, Kansas City, Missouri 64106.

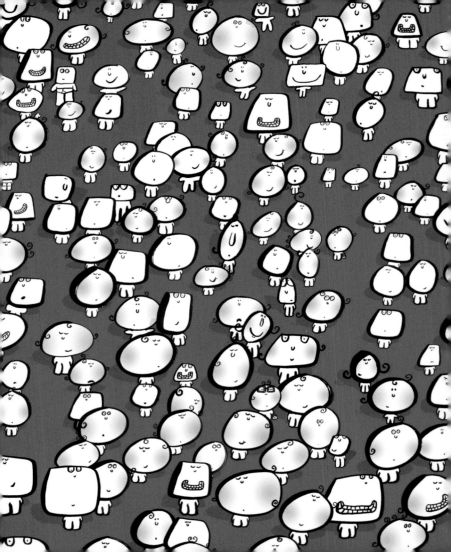